Purchase of this book is supported in whole
or part by the Institute of Museum and
Library Services through the Library
Services and Technology Act, administered by
the Oregon State Library.

Independence Public Library 2017

SCREWS

IN MY
MAKERSPACE

by Tim Miller and
Rebecca Sjonger

CRABTREE
Publishing Company
www.crabtreebooks.com

For Paul, Bart, and Greg at Fusion Labworks. Build something awesome!

Authors: Tim Miller, Rebecca Sjonger

Series research and development:
Reagan Miller

Editorial director: Kathy Middleton

Editor: Janine Deschenes

Design: Margaret Amy Salter

Proofreader: Petrice Custance

Photo research: Margaret Amy Salter

Production coordinator and prepress technician:
Margaret Amy Salter

Print coordinator: Margaret Amy Salter

Photographs:

Shutterstock: © s_oleg p6 (bottom right); © Cassiohabib p29

Craig Culliford: pp8-9

All other images by Shutterstock

Library and Archives Canada Cataloguing in Publication

Miller, Tim, 1973-, author
        Screws in my makerspace / Tim Miller, Rebecca Sjonger.

(Simple machines in my makerspace)
Includes index.
Issued in print and electronic formats.
ISBN 978-0-7787-3373-7 (hardcover).--
ISBN 978-0-7787-3381-2 (softcover).--
ISBN 978-1-4271-1903-2 (HTML)

        1. Screws--Juvenile literature. 2. Makerspaces--Juvenile literature.
I. Sjonger, Rebecca, author II. Title.

TJ1338.M55 2017   j621.8'82   C2016-907448-X
                                            C2016-907449-8

Library of Congress Cataloging-in-Publication Data

Names: Miller, Tim, 1973- author. | Sjonger, Rebecca, author.
Title: Screws in my makerspace / Tim Miller and Rebecca Sjonger.
Description: New York, New York : Crabtree Publishing Company, [2017]
   | Series: Simple machines in my makerspace | Audience: Ages 8-11. |
   Audience: Grades 4 to 6. | Includes index.
Identifiers: LCCN 2016054109 (print) | LCCN 2016056159 (ebook) |
   ISBN 9780778733737 (reinforced library binding : alk. paper) |
   ISBN 9780778733812 (pbk. : alk. paper) |
   ISBN 9781427119032 (Electronic HTML)
Subjects: LCSH: Screws--Juvenile literature. | Simple machines--Juvenile
   literature. | Makerspaces--Juvenile literature.
Classification: LCC TJ1338 .M4835 2017 (print) | LCC TJ1338 (ebook) |
   DDC 621.8/11--dc23
LC record available at https://lccn.loc.gov/2016054109

Crabtree Publishing Company
www.crabtreebooks.com   1-800-387-7650

Printed in Canada/032017/BF20170111

Published in Canada
Crabtree Publishing
616 Welland Ave.
St. Catharines, Ontario
L2M 5V6

Published in the United States
Crabtree Publishing
PMB 59051
350 Fifth Avenue, 59th Floor
New York, New York 10118

Published in the United Kingdom
Crabtree Publishing
Maritime House
Basin Road North, Hove
BN41 1WR

Published in Australia
Crabtree Publishing
3 Charles Street
Coburg North
VIC 3058

CONTENTS

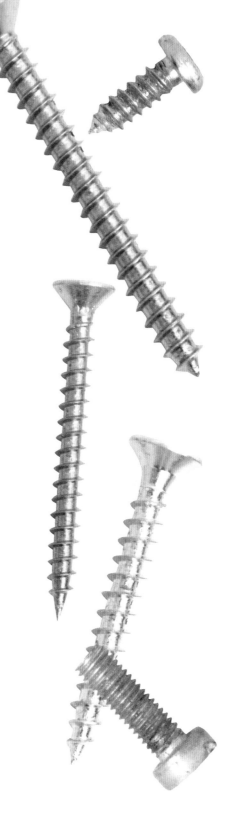

YOU CAN BE A MAKER!

Makers are people who solve problems and carry out tasks in many different creative ways. They are not afraid to experiment with ideas, even if their ideas don't work. Makers create new ways to use everyday items and use their hands to learn and create. From presses to pumps, this book will get you started on becoming a maker yourself!

TEAMWORK

Teamwork is one of the most important parts of being a maker. Working together with other makers means that you can combine ideas and points of view to create something amazing. Makers also share skills and supplies. They work together in **makerspaces**. Makerspaces can be anywhere—your school, your local library, and even at your own home!

A new way of learning

There is no right or wrong way to make something.
Makers know that:

✓ The only limit is your imagination.

✓ Every idea or question—even ones that seem silly—
could lead to something amazing.

✓ Each team member adds value to a project.

✓ Things do not always go as planned. This is part of being a maker!
Challenges help us think creatively.

WHAT IS A SCREW?

What do jar lids, car jacks, and light bulbs have in common? They use screws! There are many kinds of screws. They each have a thread, which is a raised ridge. The winding curve of the thread is a spiral. It winds around the outside of the shaft, or the longer, column-like part of the screw. Screw shafts come in many sizes.

SIMPLE MACHINES

A screw is a **simple machine**. These machines are tools with few or no moving parts. We use them to change the amount or direction of a **force**. Force is the **effort** needed to push or pull on an object. Screws can change a twisting force into a holding or squeezing force.

HELP WITH WORK

We call the use of force to move an object from one place to another **work**. Screws can make work easier, faster, or safer in many ways. For example, they can hold objects together tightly. **Bolts** are common screws with tiny amounts of space between the threads. They make it easier to join the many parts of a car.

bolts

SCREWS IN ACTION

Screws can also lift and lower loads. Have you ever sat on or seen a stool that rotates? The large screw under the seat has a lot of space between its threads. It raises or lowers the seat quickly. Other kinds of screws make holes in objects such as wood.

threads

Threads can have tight or wide spirals. The screw above has tight threads. The screw below has wider threads.

MAKE A SCREW

The activity below will help you understand the parts and function of a screw. You will learn how threads on a screw are formed and how the distance between threads affects how a screw is used. This will help you with the maker missions in this book.

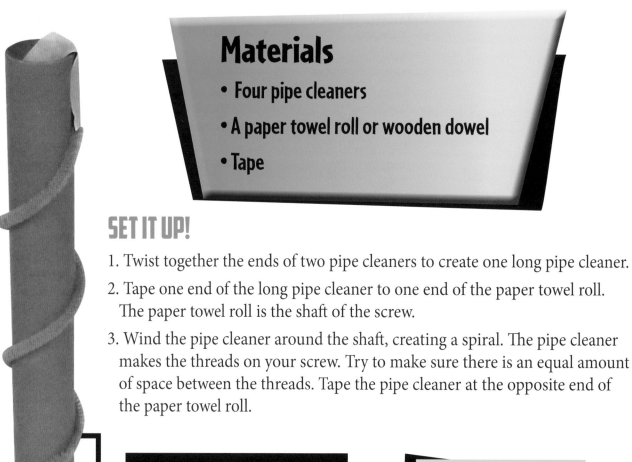

Materials
- Four pipe cleaners
- A paper towel roll or wooden dowel
- Tape

SET IT UP!

1. Twist together the ends of two pipe cleaners to create one long pipe cleaner.

2. Tape one end of the long pipe cleaner to one end of the paper towel roll. The paper towel roll is the shaft of the screw.

3. Wind the pipe cleaner around the shaft, creating a spiral. The pipe cleaner makes the threads on your screw. Try to make sure there is an equal amount of space between the threads. Tape the pipe cleaner at the opposite end of the paper towel roll.

Screw Thread #1

Winding the pipe cleaner around the shaft shows how the threads of a screw are formed.

The wider the space between the threads, the more effort it takes for a screw to turn.

4. Unravel your pipe cleaner. Twist together the ends of two more pipe cleaners, then attach them to your first two pipe cleaners. All four should now be attached together.

5. Repeat steps 2 and 3 with the longer pipe cleaner.

> A screw with less distance between its threads is easier to turn.

Think About It

Which would take longer to turn–Screw Thread #1 or Screw Thread #2? Which would take less effort to turn?

Take notice of the threads on screws you see used around you. What kinds of screws are used to hold things together? What kinds of screws are used to raise or lower things?

Once you understand how a simple machine works, you will be able to modify, or change, it to solve different problems. How you build each screw will change based on the criteria of each maker mission. For some of the maker missions in this book, you will need to use metal screws and other tools such as screwdrivers, bolts, **nuts**, and **washers**. Ask an adult to help you find these items. For help, check out the "Modify Your Machine" boxes throughout the book.

bolt

screwdriver

nut

screw

washers

MAKER TIPS

Time to get creative with screws! Kick off each of the maker projects in this book by brainstorming. Try giving yourself five minutes to come up with as many ideas as possible. If you are working with other makers, have them write down their ideas too. Be open to other points of view and respect others' ideas.

When you have a list of ideas, make a plan to create the best one. It can be helpful to measure out and draw each part of your project. Remember that your plans for the project could change as you go! Being open-minded is as important as planning.

Helpful hints

Running into problems is part of the maker process. If you are stuck, try some of the following tips:

• Think about problem-solving tools around you. **Ask:** Is there something out there that solves a similar problem?

• **Ask:** What would happen if I changed the shape, size, or strength of a material?

• Look at your list of ideas. **Ask:** Can we combine two or more ideas into one?

• Take a time out! Sometimes, taking a short break can refresh your mind and help you come back ready to work.

• Think about each part of your problem or challenge. **Ask:** Is there a certain part or area that is not working?

SCREWS THAT JOIN

Screws can make it easier to join two things together. Look at the furniture in your home or at school. You will find screws holding many parts together. Do you see them joining anything else in the room? For example, you may notice screws keeping a shelf on a wall or holding a door and hinge together.

HOW DOES IT WORK?

People twist screws into two objects to join them. The small twisting force needed to install a screw creates a larger force along the length of a screw as it turns tightly into the objects. This is what holds the two objects together solidly.

ALL KINDS OF SCREWS

Screws made for wood have pointed tips that cut into a board. Another kind of screw called a bolt has a flat tip. It goes through pre-made holes in two or more objects. A nut threads onto the bolt and presses the objects together. You could use either kind of screw in the challenge on page 14.

bolt

nut

Tools called screwdrivers are used to twist screws into hard objects. Screwdrivers have parts that fit into the top of the screw. People hold the handle of the screwdriver. They push down on the screw and twist it at the same time.

TRY IT!

Are you ready to make your own piece of furniture to help store your stuff? Remember that makers start by planning their projects. This includes brainstorming and drawing your ideas. Flip to page 14 to get started!

MAKE IT HOLD TOGETHER

Get ready to make! Build a shelf that uses screws to join at least two pieces of wood. Your shelf can stand on its own or attach to a wall. It must be strong enough to hold at least five books.

Materials

- Paper
- Pencil
- Measuring tape or ruler
- Wooden boards
- Saw (Optional material. Always use adult supervision.)
- Screws
- Screwdriver
- Hooks/hangers for the back of a shelf
- Books for testing

MODIFY YOUR MACHINE

This challenge requires metal screws and a screwdriver. Ask an adult to help you find and use these tools.

THINK ABOUT IT

Materials

Look around for materials that you could recycle in this project. Do you have any family members, friends, or neighbors with spare wood?

If you need to cut wood, find an adult to do it for you. Is there a makerspace in your community where you could get help?

Size

How will measuring help you?

What should you measure?

MISSION ACCOMPLISHED

Place five or more books on your shelf to test it. If your shelf is meant to be attached to a wall, ask an adult to help. Place five or more books on it to test it.

Did it work as you planned? If not, what could you try next? Find more ideas for your shelf on page 30.

SCREWS THAT LIFT UP AND DOWN

Some screws make it easier to lift things up and down. Have you ever flattened something, such as a flower or leaf, between two boards? You may have raised or lowered the boards together and then apart with screws. This is a press. Presses work with many different objects, such as squeezing a piece of fruit to release its juice.

HOW DOES IT WORK?

A basic press brings two flat layers together tightly. Often, a large screw twists to lower the top surface toward the bottom surface. As the top part lowers, it squeezes or flattens an object against the bottom part. The screw turns in the opposite direction to lift the top surface and release the object.

The force between the surfaces is much greater than the twisting force put on the screws, which makes the work of pressing easier.

SQUISH!

> Sometimes a flat washer goes between a bolt and nut. It helps hold them together.

MORE THAN ONE METHOD

The two layers of a press can lift up and down in a variety of ways. Some presses use two or more screws that twist at the same time. You could make holes in two layers and use bolts, for instance. Tightening nuts onto the bolts squeezes the surfaces together. Loosening them releases the pressed object.

TRY IT!

You can make your own press to see how this works. Check out the Make it Press challenge on the next page. Use your imagination as you choose your materials and design.

MAKE IT PRESS

This project could get messy! Make a press that can squeeze the juice from two kinds of fruits or vegetables. Collect the juices. Measure them to see which one held the most liquid.

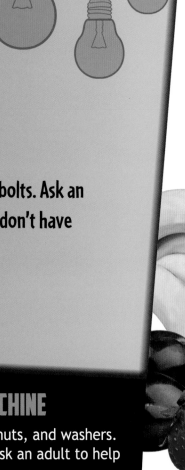

Materials

- Paper
- Pencil
- Measuring tape or ruler
- 2 long metal bolts
- 2 nuts that fit on the bolts
- 2 large washers
- 2 boards with holes in them for the bolts. Ask an adult to help you make holes if you don't have boards with holes already.
- Fruits/vegetables
- Measuring cups

MODIFY YOUR MACHINE

This project requires metal bolts, nuts, and washers. You may also need a screwdriver. Ask an adult to help you find and use these tools.

THINK ABOUT IT

Design

How will brainstorming with a team help you come up with the best possible press?

Who could help you make holes in the flat surfaces of your press? Could you ask a parent, a teacher, or an adult at a community makerspace?

Which parts do you need to sketch to be sure your ideas will work?

Materials

Where are the best places to put the bolts?

Which fruits or vegetables do you think will squeeze well? How will you collect their juices?

MISSION ACCOMPLISHED

Were you able to squeeze your test fruits or vegetables enough to collect their juices? If not, what could you try next?

If your press works well, flip to Endless Ideas on page 30 to try something new with it.

Have you ever used a see-through gumball machine? The gumballs spiral slowly down a shaft in the center of the machine. This is a great example of how screws make it easier to move objects from one location to another!

SLOW SPIRALS

When a gumball falls from the storage area at the top of a machine, force pulls it down toward the ground. Some machines have straight drops and flaps to keep gumballs from shooting out onto the floor. Using a spiral motion instead moves the gumballs over a longer distance, which slows them down and keeps them from shooting onto the floor.

HOW DOES IT WORK?

The threads in this kind of screw are what make it work well. They must be wide enough to hold the gumballs without them falling off. The slant of the thread helps keep gumballs from falling off, too. These threads also need enough space between them to allow the gumballs to fit.

TRY IT!

To see how this kind of screw works, make your own simple machine to move objects. Get some friends together and share your ideas! Working in a team can help you think of your project in new ways. Flip to the next page to get started.

MAKE IT MOVE

MAKER MISSION

Make a spiral that carries a load. Your screw must move a small ball from the top to the bottom of a shaft, without it moving too fast or falling out of the thread. The shaft must be at least 1 foot (30.5 cm) tall.

Materials

- Paper
- Pencil
- Measuring tape or ruler
- Shaft
- Base to hold up shaft, such as a paper towel holder
- Tape, glue, etc.
- Flexible material for threads, such as cut cardboard tubes or folded/curved sheets of construction paper
- Ball

MODIFY YOUR MACHINE

Your threads need to carry a small object. They will need to be made of a strong and flexible material. You may need to add sides.

THINK ABOUT IT

Materials

Is there anything around your home that already has a base, which you could use as the shaft?

Design

Which materials are flexible enough to spiral around a shaft and strong enough to hold up the ball?

Which factors do you need to keep in mind as you make your threads? Read pages 20–21 and look at the pictures again for ideas.

How could you make threads by joining multiple pieces of material?

MISSION ACCOMPLISHED

It's time to test your ball-moving machine! If it does not work as you planned, what could you try next?

Once you succeed at this challenge, go to page 30 for ideas to make it even better.

SCREWS THAT CARRY WATER

One of the earliest uses of screws was to make moving water easier and faster. Are you picturing water flowing downward like in a gumball machine? Screws are actually used to move water upward. A screw pump carries water from one level up to a higher level. Archimedes dreamed up this kind of screw. He was a Greek inventor who lived over 2,000 years ago.

Archimedes

HOW DOES IT WORK?

A screw pump scoops up water from the source. That source could be anything from a lake to a small pail. As the screw turns, water is picked up by the threads at the bottom and moved up the shaft to the top. The threads are made in a way that holds in the water. Check out the diagram below to see how this works.

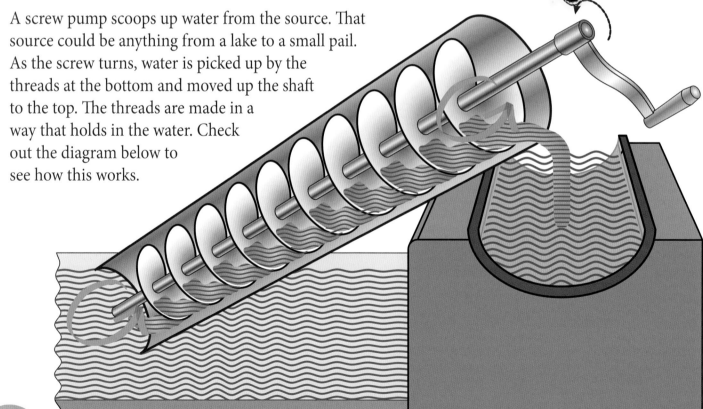

THREAD POWER

The threads can be inside or outside of the shaft in a screw pump. They can also be different widths and materials. For example, threads on the outside of a shaft may use bendy plastic tubes that hold in the water. The closer together the threads are, the longer the water must travel.

TRY IT!

Flip the page to get started on your own screw pump project. It may not be easy, but makers are always up for a challenge!

Are you ready to make your own screw pump? Your creation must move 1 cup (237 ml) of water from one container to a higher container—without spilling any!

Materials

- Paper
- Pencil
- Measuring tape or ruler
- Shaft
- Threads, such as plastic tubing or connected bendable straws
- Tape, glue, etc.
- 1 cup (237 ml) of water
- 2 containers

MODIFY YOUR MACHINE

To make your screw pump threads, choose materials with a curved surface or add sides. You may need to build a structure around your screw so water does not spill out.

THINK ABOUT IT

Materials

Do you want to see the water as it moves? If so, how does that affect the materials you use?

 Size

What materials will you choose to keep the water inside the thread?

How will the amounts of space you leave between the threads change how the water moves?

Experiment with different heights for the top level of your pump. Usually, screw pumps are placed on an angle. How steep should it be?

Design

How will you catch the water at the top?

What difference will the width of the tubing make?

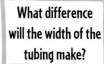

MISSION ACCOMPLISHED

Test your screw pump to see if you can move 1 cup (237 ml) of water upward without spilling any of it. Make notes about anything that you need to change.

Once your pump works well, try something new. Find some ideas on page 30.

MORE MACHINES

There are five other kinds of simple machines. Which of the following simple machines have you used or seen before?

NAME	PURPOSE	PICTURE	EXAMPLES
inclined planes	move objects between two heights		water slide funnel wheelchair ramp
levers	move, lift, or lower objects		seesaw scissors catapult
pulleys	lift, lower, or move objects; transfer force from one object to another		flagpole zip line bicycle chain
wedges	split apart or lift objects; stop objects from moving		ax door stop shovel
wheels and axles	move objects		Ferris wheel rolling pin skateboard

COMPLEX MACHINES

Joining two or more simple machines creates a **complex machine**. Screws are in most complex machines because they have so many uses. Bicycles, cranes, and roller coasters are just a few examples. Can you think of more ideas?

A roller coaster combines many simple machines, such as screws to hold its parts together and inclined planes to get the coaster rolling!

CHANGE IT UP!

How could you use a screw and another simple machine to make a complex machine? Start by experimenting with one of the projects from this book. Flip to page 30 for more project inspiration.

ENDLESS IDEAS

Makers are always learning and coming up with new ideas! You could make each of the projects in this book in many different ways. For example:

Make It Hold Together (pages 14–15):

- How could you change your shelf to hold 10 books?
- What would you need to do to add a second shelf to your project, and hold even more books?

Make It Press (pages 18–19):

- Could you add handles to the heads of your bolts? How?
- What difference does this make in how you use your press? Is your press strong enough to crush other items? Try it out!

Make It Move (pages 22-23):

- Which materials would you change to improve how your spiral moves the ball?
- How could you double the length of the shaft?

Make It Flow (pages 26-27):

- Which modifications would allow you to move double the amount of water in the same time? Is it even possible? Try it!

LEARNING MORE

BOOKS

Bailey, Gerry. *Winding Around: The Screw.* Crabtree, 2014.

Challen, Paul. *Get to Know Screws.* Crabtree, 2009.

De Medeiros, Michael. *Simple Machines: Screws.* Weigl, 2013.

Sirota, Lyn. *Screws.* The Child's World, 2014.

• •

WEBSITES

Watch an animated video about screws at the Mocomi website.
http://mocomi.com/screw

Visit this link for a more in-depth look at the Archimedes screw pump.
http://bit.ly/2fbDJ0R

Play games, learn more about simple machines, and find other great resources at the Idaho Public Television website.
http://idahoptv.org/sciencetrek/topics/simple_machines/facts.cfm

• •

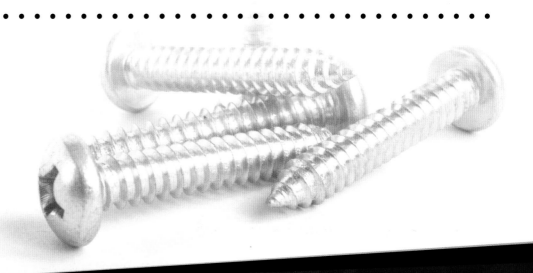

GLOSSARY

bolt A kind of screw with a flat tip and tight threads

car jack A machine that makes the work of lifting up a car faster, easier, and safer

complex machine A machine that combines at least two simple machines

effort The amount of energy, or power, used to do something

flexible Describes something that bends without breaking

force The effort needed to push or pull on an object

makerspace A place where makers work together and share their ideas and resources

nut A metal ring that is threaded onto a bolt to hold things together

press A machine that squeezes an object tightly

pump A machine that moves liquids such as water

screw A simple machine that has a thread which spirals around a straight shaft

shaft The column-like center of a screw

simple machine A tool with few or no moving parts that people use to change the amount or direction of a force

spiral A winding curve shape

thread The raised spiral on the outside of a screw's shaft

washer A thin, flat metal plate that is placed between a nut and a bolt to help fasten a load

work The use of force to move an object from one place to another

INDEX

ABOUT THE AUTHORS

Tim Miller is a mechanical engineer who loves to work with his hands. He is also a founding board member of Fusion Labworks, a maker community. Rebecca Sjonger is the author of over 40 children's books, including three titles in the *Be a Maker!* series.